Mastering SQL

The Ultimate Guide for Beginners and Professionals

Basil U.

COPYRIGHT PAGE

All right reserved. No part of this publication may be published in any means or by any form, either by photocopying, scanning or otherwise without any prior written permission from the copyright holder.

Copyright © 2024 Basil U.

About the Author

Basil is a software engineer based in Dubai, United Arab Emirate, he has worked as a Developer for over 8 years and has been building dynamic web applications, for personal and for companies world wide.

In the time past his experience has helped different kinds of companies ranging from startups to large scale enterprises. He is also vast in knowledge with Cloud Computation, Mobile Application Development, AI Integration, API Integration and Databases.

I am grateful to my family who has been a huge support to me since I started writing this book. Thanks to my wife Onyi and children for their endless support.

Content

Introduction to SQL and Databases

Chapter One

SQL Fundamentals

Chapter Two

Understanding and Designing Database Structures

Chapter Three

Filtering and Sorting Data for Business Insights

Chapter Four

Aggregations and Grouping

Chapter Five

Joining Tables to Find Meaningful Connections

Chapter Six

SQL Best Practices for Efficiency and Security

Chapter Seven

Advanced SQL Techniques

Introduction to SQL and Daabases

1.1 What is SQL?

SQL (Structured Query Language) is a programming language used to manage and manipulate data in relational databases. Developed in the 1970s, SQL has since become the standard for querying, inserting, updating, and deleting data within databases. It's also crucial in database administration, where it helps structure and control access to large datasets. SQL has been widely adopted across industries for its effectiveness in handling structured data, making it one of the most widely used languages in data science, software engineering, and business analytics.

In simpler terms, SQL allows users to communicate with databases to:

- Retrieve data (e.g., list all orders made by a customer).
- Modify data (e.g., update a customer's address).

- Structure data (e.g., define tables and relationships).
- Control data access and optimize performance.

1.2 Why SQL Matters in Today's World

Data is often described as "the new oil" because it fuels critical decisions and strategic directions for businesses worldwide. SQL is the tool that makes it possible to access, analyze, and manage this data. Today's digital economy relies on SQL to power e-commerce platforms, social media, content management systems, and business intelligence tools.

Imagine a company like Amazon: its database tracks millions of customer transactions, product listings, and supplier details. SQL enables Amazon to efficiently retrieve, process, and manage this data, supporting everything from customer recommendations to supply chain optimization.

Real-World Applications of SQL:

- **Retail and E-commerce:** Managing inventory, tracking orders, customer data, and sales.
- **Banking and Finance:** Monitoring transactions, managing accounts, generating reports.
- **Healthcare:** Storing patient records, tracking medical history, optimizing hospital resources.
- **Social Media:** User profiles, posts, friend relationships, messages.
- **Logistics:** Tracking shipments, optimizing delivery routes, managing inventory across locations.

1.3 What are Databases?

At the heart of SQL is the database—a structured collection of data organized to be easily accessed, managed, and updated. Databases are built to store vast amounts of data while maintaining efficiency and security.

Types of Databases

There are several types of databases, each with a specific purpose. The most common are:

- **Relational Databases (RDBMS):** These are structured databases based on the relational model, where data is stored in tables with rows and columns. SQL is the primary language for relational databases, which include popular systems like MySQL, PostgreSQL, Oracle, and Microsoft SQL Server.
- **NoSQL Databases:** These databases are designed for flexibility, storing unstructured or semi-structured data. Examples include MongoDB, Cassandra, and Redis. While SQL is not typically used in NoSQL databases, they often incorporate querying languages specific to the database.

1.4 Key Database Concepts

Tables and Records

- **Tables:** The basic structure for storing data in a relational database, often resembling an Excel sheet. A table contains rows (records) and columns (fields).
- **Records (Rows):** Each record represents a unique entry in the table. For instance, each row in a "Customers" table might represent a single customer.

Primary and Foreign Keys

- **Primary Key:** A unique identifier for each record in a table. It could be an ID number or any field guaranteed to be unique.
- **Foreign Key:** A field in one table that links to the primary key in another table. This connection allows tables to relate and ensures data consistency.

1.5 Getting Started with SQL Databases: Setup and Tools

To start using SQL, you need access to a database. Here are a few user-friendly and accessible database options:

MySQL and MariaDB

MySQL is one of the most popular open-source relational database management systems (RDBMs). You can download it from [MySQL's official website](#) or use a compatible version like [MariaDB](#), which is also open source.

PostgreSQL

PostgreSQL is another powerful, open-source RDBMS known for its scalability and support for complex queries. It's favored for data-heavy applications. Download it at [PostgreSQL's official site](#).

SQLite

SQLite is a lightweight, serverless SQL database that works well for smaller projects. It doesn't require a complex setup, making it an excellent choice for learners and embedded applications. SQLite comes preinstalled with Python and is available at [SQLite's website](#).

1.6 Installing MySQL (Example Setup)

Here's a step-by-step guide to installing MySQL to get you started:

1. **Download**: Visit [MySQL's download page](#). Choose your operating system and download the appropriate installer.
2. **Install**: Run the installer and follow the on-screen instructions. Select the configuration options suitable for your needs (default settings work well for most users).

3. **Set up MySQL Workbench**: During installation, you can also install MySQL Workbench, an integrated tool for SQL development and administration. MySQL Workbench provides a user-friendly interface for managing databases and running SQL queries.

Once installed, you can log in to your MySQL database with the following command:

```
mysql -u root -p
```

This command opens the MySQL prompt, where you can start writing SQL commands.

1.7 Writing Your First SQL Query

Example: Creating a Database and Table

Let's start by creating a simple database and a table.

1. **Create a Database:**

```
CREATE DATABASE shop;
```

Use the Database:

```sql
USE shop;
```

Create a Table:

```sql
CREATE TABLE products (
    product_id INT PRIMARY KEY,
    name VARCHAR(100),
    price DECIMAL(10, 2),
    in_stock BOOLEAN
);
```

In this example, we've created a database called `shop` and a `products` table with columns `product_id`, `name`, `price`, and `in_stock`. Each product will have an ID, a name, a price, and an indication of whether it's in stock.

Inserting Data into the Table

Let's add some sample data into our `products` table:

```sql
INSERT INTO products (product_id, name, price, in_stock)
VALUES (1, 'Laptop', 999.99, TRUE),
       (2, 'Smartphone', 599.99, TRUE),
       (3, 'Headphones', 199.99, FALSE);
```

Querying the Data

To view the data in your table, use the `SELECT` statement:

```sql
SELECT * FROM products;
```

This command retrieves all records from the `products` table.

1.8 Practical Use Case: Creating a Customer Management Database

To make this practical, let's imagine we're building a customer management database for a small business. This database will have tables like `Customers`, `Orders`, and `Products`.

Create the Customers Table:

```sql
CREATE TABLE customers (
    customer_id INT PRIMARY KEY,
    first_name VARCHAR(50),
    last_name VARCHAR(50),
    email VARCHAR(100),
    phone VARCHAR(15),
    join_date DATE
);
```

Create the Orders Table:

```sql
CREATE TABLE orders (
    order_id INT PRIMARY KEY,
    customer_id INT,
    order_date DATE,
    amount DECIMAL(10, 2),
    FOREIGN KEY (customer_id) REFERENCES customers(customer_id)
);
```

With these tables, we can now start inserting data, querying relationships, and analyzing customer purchase behaviors.

1.9 Practice Exercises

1. **Basic Queries**: Write SQL commands to add customers and view customer details.
2. **Modify Data**: Update a customer's information using the `UPDATE` statement.
3. **Delete Data**: Remove an order or customer record with `DELETE`.
4. **Join Tables**: Use `JOIN` to link `customers` with `orders` and get purchase history.

1.10 Key Takeaways

- SQL is an essential tool for managing and interacting with relational databases.
- Databases organize data efficiently, supporting use cases across virtually all sectors.

- This chapter provided the foundation for writing and executing SQL commands and creating simple databases.

Chapter One

SQL Fundamentals

1. Introduction to SQL Basics

- **What is SQL?**
  SQL (Structured Query Language) is a standardized language used to manage and manipulate relational databases. It is the primary tool for handling data in databases, allowing users to retrieve, update, insert, and delete data efficiently.

- **Why Learn SQL?**
  With data at the core of business decision-making, SQL is an essential tool for analysts, developers, and business professionals alike. SQL knowledge helps in organizing data to derive actionable insights, and it's a valuable skill across tech and non-tech roles.

2. Setting Up Your Environment

- **Choosing Your SQL Database**
  Overview of popular SQL databases: MySQL, PostgreSQL, SQLite, and SQL Server.
    - **Referral Links:** Include affiliate links to services like Amazon RDS or DigitalOcean to help readers get started with SQL in the cloud.

- **Installation and Setup**
  Step-by-step instructions to install MySQL or PostgreSQL.
    - **Connecting to the Database:** Using command-line or graphical tools (e.g., DBeaver or pgAdmin).
    - **Creating Your First Database:** Walkthrough on setting up a basic database to use in examples.

3. **SQL Query Basics: Structure and Syntax**

- **Understanding SQL Syntax**
  SQL commands are structured in clear segments:
    - Keywords (e.g., `SELECT`, `FROM`, `WHERE`)
    - Clauses (like `WHERE`, `ORDER BY`)
    - Operators (`=`, `>`, `<`)
    - Comments (explaining queries)

4. **The `SELECT` Statement: Retrieving Data**

- **Syntax**
  The `SELECT` statement is the foundation of data retrieval in SQL.
    - Example: `SELECT column_name FROM table_name;`

- **Selecting Specific Columns**
    - Example: Selecting specific fields in a customer table (`first_name`, `last_name`, `email`).
    - Real-world use case: Customer support retrieves basic customer info for verification purposes.
- **Selecting All Columns**
    - Using `SELECT *` to retrieve all columns.
    - Pros and cons: It's convenient but can be resource-heavy if overused in large tables.

5. The `WHERE` Clause: Filtering Data

- **Why Use `WHERE`?**
    Allows for targeted data retrieval by specifying conditions.
    - Syntax: `SELECT * FROM table_name WHERE condition;`
- **Basic Operators in `WHERE` Clauses**
    - `=`: Exact matches
    - `<>` or `!=`: Not equal
    - `>` and `<`: Greater than or less than
    - Example: `SELECT * FROM customers WHERE age > 30;`

Real-World Scenario: Filtering Sales Data

Example of using `WHERE` to view sales above a certain dollar amount:

sql

```sql
SELECT * FROM sales WHERE amount > 500;
```

6. Using the `ORDER BY` Clause: Sorting Results

- **Syntax and Importance**

    `ORDER BY` organizes query results in ascending (`ASC`) or descending (`DESC`) order.

Example:
sql

```sql
SELECT first_name, last_name FROM employees ORDER BY last_name ASC;
```

Real-World Scenario: Sorting by Customer Spend

Sorting results to identify top customers based on purchase amounts.

sql

```sql
SELECT customer_id, amount FROM transactions ORDER BY amount DESC;
```

7. Practical Exercise 1: Creating a Basic Query

- **Scenario:** Pulling a list of active customers from a `customers` table.

Step-by-Step Guide

Sample query to retrieve only active customers with order totals above $100:

sql
```
SELECT first_name, last_name, total_spent FROM customers WHERE status = 'active' AND total_spent > 100;
```

- **Explanation:** Walk through each part of the query, explaining how SQL retrieves, filters, and orders data.

8. The `INSERT INTO` Statement: Adding Data

- **Syntax and Use**

  `INSERT INTO` adds new rows to a table.

Basic Syntax:

sql
```
INSERT INTO table_name (column1, column2, column3)
VALUES (value1, value2, value3);
```

Inserting Multiple Rows

Bulk insert of rows for data initialization:

sql

```
INSERT INTO employees (first_name, last_name, role) VALUES ('Alice', 'Smith', 'Developer'), ('Bob', 'Jones', 'Manager');
```

9. Practical Exercise 2: Adding New Records

- Scenario: Adding new products to an inventory.

Instructions and Example

A step-by-step guide on adding records to an `inventory` table:

sql

```
INSERT INTO inventory (product_name, price, quantity) VALUES ('Laptop', 799.99, 50);
```

10. The UPDATE Statement: Modifying Data

- Syntax and Real-World Use Cases
  Modify existing data, such as updating prices or customer contact information.

Basic Syntax:

sql

```
UPDATE table_name SET column1 = value1, column2 = value2 WHERE condition;
```

Practical Example: Price Update

Increase prices by 5% for a specific category:

sql

```sql
UPDATE products SET price = price * 1.05 WHERE category = 'Electronics';
```

11. The DELETE Statement: Removing Data

- **Syntax and Precautions**
  Delete removes rows that meet specified conditions.

Basic Syntax:

sql

```sql
DELETE FROM table_name WHERE condition;
```

Example: Cleaning Out Old Records

Removing inactive users from the database:

sql

```sql
DELETE FROM users WHERE status = 'inactive' AND last_login < '2023-01-01';
```

- **Real-World Scenario: Data Retention Policies**
  Ensuring that records are deleted as per regulatory standards, using SQL queries to automate this.

12. Combining Clauses for Complex Queries

Using AND and OR in Conditions

Combine multiple conditions in WHERE clauses.

sql

```sql
SELECT * FROM customers WHERE age > 30 AND country = 'USA';
```

- **Chaining Conditions for Advanced Filtering**
  Scenarios where multiple conditions can refine data retrieval.

13. Practical Exercise 3: Creating a Simple Report

- Scenario: Generating a customer report filtered by region and sorted by purchase volume.

Step-by-Step Guide

Guide readers to write a combined query using SELECT, WHERE, and ORDER BY:

sql

```sql
SELECT first_name, last_name, country, total_spent FROM customers WHERE country = 'Canada' ORDER BY total_spent DESC;
```

14. Summary: Wrapping Up SQL Basics

- A recap of the core SQL commands (`SELECT`, `INSERT`, `UPDATE`, `DELETE`).
- Reinforce the importance of `WHERE` for filtering and `ORDER BY` for sorting.
- Final Exercise: Give readers a combined task to practice all learned commands.

15. Additional Resources and Recommended Tools

- List useful online resources, tutorials, and practice platforms.
- Referral Links: Link to SQL course providers, database hosting solutions, and tools for hands-on practice.

Chapter Two

Understanding and Designing Database Structures

Introduction to Database Design

Start by introducing the importance of database design. Explain that a well-designed database is essential for efficient data management, ensuring data consistency, and supporting future growth without compromising performance.

> **Example Scenario:** Imagine you're designing a database for a small online store. This database should store customer information, product details, orders, and order items. A poorly designed structure could lead to duplicate information, inconsistencies, and slower query performance as the database grows.

1. Key Concepts in Database Design

- **Data Organization**: Explain how a relational database organizes data into tables, each representing a specific type of entity.
- **Entities and Attributes**: Define entities as real-world objects, such as "Customer" or "Order," and attributes as characteristics of these entities, like `name`, `email`, or `order_date`.
- **Primary Keys**: Introduce primary keys as unique identifiers for records in a table, emphasizing their role in maintaining data integrity.
  - *Example*: In a "Customer" table, the primary key could be `customer_id`.
- **Foreign Keys**: Define foreign keys as fields in a table that reference primary keys in other tables, establishing relationships between data.
  - *Example*: In an "Order" table, `customer_id` might be a foreign key linking each order to a specific customer.

2. Understanding Relationships in Database Design

- **One-to-One Relationships**: Explain with examples, like a table where each user has one unique profile.
- **One-to-Many Relationships**: Most common relationship, where one entity relates to many others (e.g., one customer can place multiple orders).
- **Many-to-Many Relationships**: Describe scenarios like "Students and Courses," where each student can enroll in multiple courses and each course has multiple students.
    - Show how to create junction tables to handle many-to-many relationships.

3. Creating a Database Schema for Real-World Applications

- **Scenario-Based Example**: Designing an Online Store Database
    - *Customer Table*: Define columns such as `customer_id`, `first_name`, `last_name`, `email`, and `phone`.

- *Product Table*: Define `product_id`, `name`, `description`, `price`, and `stock`.
- *Order Table*: Columns might include `order_id`, `order_date`, and `customer_id` as a foreign key.
- *OrderItems Table*: This table will include `order_item_id`, `order_id`, `product_id`, and `quantity`, creating a connection between orders and products.

4. Normalization: Ensuring Database Efficiency

- First Normal Form (1NF): Explain the basics—ensuring each column holds atomic values with no repeating groups.
- Second Normal Form (2NF): Focus on removing partial dependencies. For instance, describe a situation where each non-primary key column should depend on the entire primary key.

- **Third Normal Form (3NF):** Describe removing transitive dependencies, where non-primary columns should depend only on the primary key.
    - *Example:* In an "Orders" table, ensure columns like `customer_name` are stored in the "Customers" table instead of repeating them in "Orders."

5: Denormalization and When to Use It

- Define denormalization as a process where data redundancy is intentionally introduced to improve read performance.
- Examples of when denormalization is beneficial, such as in large reporting systems where query speed is crucial.

6: Implementing Indexes for Faster Access

- Explain what indexes are and how they speed up data retrieval.
- Describe different types of indexes, like clustered and non-clustered, and when to use them.

- *Practical Tip*: Recommend creating indexes on frequently queried columns, such as primary and foreign keys.

7. Designing for Scalability

- Discuss concepts like partitioning, sharding, and replication to prepare databases for scaling up as data grows.
- *Example*: For an e-commerce site, explain how tables can be partitioned by date to make recent transactions more accessible.

8. Practical Exercise: Building a Simple Database Schema

Provide a step-by-step practical exercise to create a schema from scratch.

Exercise Overview: The user builds an "Inventory Management System" for a warehouse.

- **Step 1**: Define the tables for `Product`, `Supplier`, and `Inventory`.
- **Step 2**: Set up primary and foreign keys.

- **Step 3**: Normalize data to 3NF.
- **Step 4**: Add indexes on key columns.
- **Step 5**: Test with sample data, running queries to check relationships and data consistency.

9. Testing and Validating the Database Design

- Outline methods to verify the design, like sample queries and data validation.
- Use examples, such as checking that an order cannot exist without a customer or that inventory levels do not allow negative stock.

10. Common Database Design Mistakes and How to Avoid Them

- Describe typical mistakes like redundant data, incorrect use of relationships, and missing indexes.
- Provide best practices to avoid each issue, using relatable examples to clarify the points.

Chapter Three

Filtering and Sorting Data for Business Insights

Outline

1. Introduction to Filtering and Sorting in SQL
   - Importance of data filtering and sorting in business insights.
   - Overview of common SQL clauses for filtering and sorting (`WHERE`, `ORDER BY`, and `LIMIT`).
2. Using the `WHERE` Clause for Precise Data Selection
   - Explanation and syntax of the `WHERE` clause.
   - Real-world examples:
     - Filtering orders based on date.
     - Retrieving customer records with specific attributes.
3. Logical Operators in Filtering: `AND`, `OR`, and `NOT`
   - Syntax and examples of `AND`, `OR`, and `NOT`.

- Practical application:
  - Filtering data with multiple conditions.
  - Combining filters to narrow down results effectively.

4. Comparison Operators for Data Retrieval
   - Overview of `=`, `<`, `>`, `<=`, `>=`, and `<>`.
   - Real-world scenario: Selecting records based on numerical data (e.g., order amounts, dates).

5. Using the IN and BETWEEN Operators
   - Explanation of `IN` and `BETWEEN`.
   - Practical application:
     - Retrieving specific values or ranges of data.
     - Example use case: Fetching orders within a date range.

6. Sorting Data with the ORDER BY Clause
   - Overview of sorting and syntax of `ORDER BY`.
   - Sorting data in ascending and descending order.

- Example scenario: Sorting products by price, customer list alphabetically.

7. **Limiting Results with the LIMIT Clause**
    - Syntax and explanation of `LIMIT`.
    - Use cases in data reporting (e.g., top-selling products, most recent transactions).

8. **Case Study: Analyzing Sales Data for Business Insights**
    - Sample dataset and problem statement.
    - Step-by-step SQL queries to demonstrate filtering and sorting.
    - Summary of business insights gained.

9. **Conclusion**
    - Recap of filtering and sorting techniques.
    - Importance of combining these techniques for meaningful data analysis.

Chapter Content (Detailed)

1. Introduction to Filtering and Sorting in SQL

In the world of data management, raw data is rarely used directly; instead, it's essential to find patterns and trends hidden within the numbers. Filtering and sorting data allow analysts and decision-makers to narrow down vast amounts of information and identify actionable insights.

Example Use Case:

Imagine you're working for an online retail company with a database of thousands of orders. To determine which products perform well, you might need to retrieve the top 10 products based on sales in the last quarter. To accomplish this, you can use SQL filtering and sorting to specify date ranges, customer regions, and sort by sales volume.

SQL provides powerful clauses like `WHERE`, `ORDER BY`, and `LIMIT` to filter and sort data with precision, making it a key tool for extracting business insights from database records.

2. Using the WHERE Clause for Precise Data Selection

The WHERE clause in SQL is fundamental to filtering data based on specific conditions. By specifying a condition in the WHERE clause, we can focus only on rows that meet the criteria, which is particularly useful in data analysis.

Syntax:

sql
```
SELECT column1, column2
FROM table_name
WHERE condition;
```

Example:

To retrieve a list of customers from the "Customers" table who live in "California," we could use the following query:

sql

```
SELECT first_name, last_name, city, state
FROM Customers
WHERE state = 'California';
```

Real-World Application:

Filtering data by specific attributes, like region, date, or category, can help answer questions such as, "Which customers have purchased a product in the last 30 days?" or "Which products belong to a particular category?"

3. Logical Operators in Filtering: AND, OR, and NOT

The `AND`, `OR`, and `NOT` operators allow for more complex filtering by combining multiple conditions within the `WHERE` clause:

- `AND` requires all conditions to be true.
- `OR` requires at least one condition to be true.
- `NOT` negates a condition.

Example:

To retrieve orders placed by customers in California or New York, but only if the order total exceeds $500, use:

sql

```sql
SELECT order_id, customer_id, total_amount
FROM Orders
WHERE (state = 'California' OR state = 'New York')
AND total_amount > 500;
```

Practical Application:

This type of filtering can be useful in scenarios where you need to analyze high-value customers in specific regions.

4. Comparison Operators for Data Retrieval

Comparison operators are integral to filtering numerical or date-based data. The most common ones include:

- =, <, >, <=, >=, and <> (not equal).

Example:

Suppose we need to find customers who have spent more than $1,000 in total.

sql

```sql
SELECT customer_id, total_spent
FROM Customers
WHERE total_spent > 1000;
```

This simple filtering technique enables companies to identify high-value customers and target them for loyalty programs or special offers.

5. Using the IN and BETWEEN Operators

The `IN` and `BETWEEN` operators offer shortcuts for filtering data based on multiple values or ranges.

- `IN` checks if a value matches any value in a list.

- `BETWEEN` specifies a range.

Example Using `IN`: To fetch orders from multiple specific states:

```sql
SELECT order_id, state
FROM Orders
WHERE state IN ('California', 'Texas', 'New York');
```

Example Using BETWEEN:

To find orders placed within a specific date range:

```sql
SELECT order_id, order_date
FROM Orders
WHERE order_date BETWEEN '2024-01-01' AND '2024-03-31';
```

Real-World Application:

This approach is particularly useful for seasonal or promotional analysis, allowing businesses to identify patterns in sales by filtering specific time frames or regions.

6. Sorting Data with the ORDER BY Clause

The ORDER BY clause enables data sorting based on specified columns in ascending (ASC) or descending (DESC) order.

Syntax:

```sql
SELECT column1, column2
FROM table_name
ORDER BY column1 ASC, column2 DESC;
```

Example:

To retrieve the top products by sales volume in descending order:

```sql
SELECT product_name, sales_volume
FROM Products
ORDER BY sales_volume DESC;
```

Real-World Scenario:

Sorting data can help businesses quickly identify top performers, track trends, or organize data in a way that highlights important information.

7. Limiting Results with the LIMIT Clause

The `LIMIT` clause restricts the number of rows returned, which is useful when only a subset of data is required.

Syntax:

sql
```
SELECT column1, column2
FROM table_name
LIMIT number_of_rows;
```

Example:

To fetch the top 5 customers by spending:

sql
```
SELECT customer_id, total_spent
FROM Customers
ORDER BY total_spent DESC
LIMIT 5;
```

8. Case Study: Analyzing Sales Data for Business Insights

Imagine we need to analyze sales data to understand customer purchasing patterns, top-performing products, and sales by region. Here's a step-by-step analysis:

1. **Retrieve high-value orders:** Orders over $1,000 in value.
2. **Identify top products:** Products with the highest sales volume.
3. **Analyze region-specific sales:** Compare sales by state or region.

Using a sequence of `WHERE`, `ORDER BY`, and `LIMIT` queries, we can uncover insights like high-value customers, top products, and regional preferences.

9. Conclusion

Filtering and sorting are essential skills for data analysis in SQL. By mastering these techniques, you can transform raw data into meaningful insights that inform strategic business decisions.

Chapter Four

Aggregations and Grouping

SQL is a powerful language for managing databases, and one of its most useful features is the ability to perform data aggregation and summarization. Aggregation allows you to analyze large sets of data and extract meaningful insights. This chapter will guide you through the fundamentals of aggregation in SQL and explore practical examples that will help you apply these concepts in real-world scenarios.

Understanding Aggregation in SQL

Aggregation refers to the process of summarizing data in a database to provide useful statistics or insights. This is typically achieved using aggregate functions. These functions perform a calculation on a set of values and return a single value. For example, you might want to find the total sales in a month, the average salary of employees in a department, or the number of customers who have made purchases.

SQL provides several built-in aggregate functions:

- COUNT(): Counts the number of rows that match a specified condition.
- SUM(): Adds up the values in a specified column.
- AVG(): Calculates the average value of a numeric column.
- MIN(): Returns the smallest value in a specified column.
- MAX(): Returns the largest value in a specified column.

These functions are usually used in conjunction with the SELECT statement to retrieve summarized data from one or more tables. Let's take a closer look at these aggregate functions and how they can be applied to real-world scenarios.

The COUNT() Function: Counting Rows

The COUNT() function is one of the most commonly used aggregate functions in SQL. It counts the number of rows that match a specific condition. You can use

`COUNT()` to calculate things like how many products are in stock, how many customers have placed an order, or how many employees are in a department.

Example 1: Counting Total Customers

Let's say you have a `customers` table with the following columns: `customer_id`, `first_name`, `last_name`, `email`, and `phone_number`. You can use `COUNT()` to find out how many customers are in your database.

sql

```sql
SELECT COUNT(*) AS total_customers
FROM customers;
```

In this example, `COUNT(*)` counts all rows in the `customers` table, and the result is aliased as `total_customers`. The output will give you the total number of customers.

Example 2: Counting Customers Who Made a Purchase

If you want to count only the customers who have made a purchase, you would use a `WHERE` clause to filter the data.

sql

```sql
SELECT COUNT(DISTINCT customer_id) AS total_customers_with_purchases
FROM orders
WHERE order_date >= '2023-01-01';
```

In this query, `COUNT(DISTINCT customer_id)` counts the number of unique customers who have made a purchase after January 1st, 2023.

The `SUM()` Function: Adding Values

The `SUM()` function is used to calculate the total sum of values in a numeric column. This can be useful for calculating things like total sales, total inventory value, or the total amount of money spent by customers.

Example 1: Summing Total Sales

Imagine you have an `orders` table with the following columns: `order_id`, `customer_id`, `order_date`, and `total_amount`. You can use `SUM()` to calculate the total sales for a specific period:

sql
```
SELECT SUM(total_amount) AS total_sales
FROM orders
WHERE order_date >= '2023-01-01';
```

In this example, `SUM(total_amount)` adds up the values in the `total_amount` column, providing the total sales for all orders placed after January 1st, 2023.

Example 2: Summing Sales by Product

If you have a `products` table and an `order_items` table that stores the quantity and price of each product in an order, you can calculate the total sales for each product:

```sql
SELECT p.product_name, SUM(oi.quantity *
oi.unit_price) AS total_sales
FROM order_items oi
JOIN products p ON oi.product_id = p.product_id
GROUP BY p.product_name;
```

This query calculates the total sales for each product by multiplying the `quantity` by the `unit_price` for each order item. The `GROUP BY` clause groups the results by product name, so you get a total sales figure for each product.

The `AVG()` Function: Calculating Averages

The `AVG()` function calculates the average value of a numeric column. This is useful when you need to find things like the average order value, the average salary in a department, or the average rating of a product.

Example 1: Calculating the Average Order Value

If you want to find the average value of orders placed by customers, you can use the `AVG()` function. For example:

sql
```sql
SELECT AVG(total_amount) AS average_order_value
FROM orders;
```

This query calculates the average value of all orders in the `orders` table.

Example 2: Calculating the Average Salary by Department

You can also use `AVG()` to calculate the average salary of employees within different departments. Assuming you have an `employees` table with columns `employee_id`, `department_id`, and `salary`, you can calculate the average salary per department.

sql
```sql
SELECT department_id, AVG(salary) AS average_salary
FROM employees
GROUP BY department_id;
```

This query calculates the average salary for each department by grouping employees by their `department_id`.

The `MIN()` and `MAX()` Functions: Finding Extremes

The `MIN()` and `MAX()` functions return the smallest and largest values, respectively, in a specified column. These functions are useful for finding things like the minimum and maximum sales, the lowest and highest prices, or the earliest and latest order dates.

Example 1: Finding the Minimum and Maximum Order Values

If you want to find the lowest and highest order values, you can use `MIN()` and `MAX()`.

```sql
SELECT MIN(total_amount) AS min_order_value,
MAX(total_amount) AS max_order_value
FROM orders;
```

This query returns the smallest and largest values in the `total_amount` column of the `orders` table.

Example 2: Finding the Earliest and Latest Order Dates

You can also use `MIN()` and `MAX()` to find the earliest and latest dates in a date column. For example, to find the first and last orders placed by customers:

```sql
SELECT MIN(order_date) AS first_order_date,
MAX(order_date) AS last_order_date
FROM orders;
```

Grouping Data: The `GROUP BY` Clause

While aggregate functions summarize individual columns, the `GROUP BY` clause allows you to group rows based on the values of one or more columns. This is essential for performing aggregations over subsets of data, such as calculating total sales by product category, or finding the average salary by department.

Example 1: Grouping Sales by Product

If you want to calculate the total sales for each product, you can use the `GROUP BY` clause to group the results by `product_name` and use the `SUM()` function to calculate the total sales for each product:

sql
```
SELECT product_name, SUM(total_amount) AS total_sales
FROM order_items oi
JOIN products p ON oi.product_id = p.product_id
GROUP BY product_name;
```

This query groups the sales by `product_name` and calculates the total sales for each product.

Example 2: Grouping Employees by Department

You can also use `GROUP BY` to calculate the average salary within each department.

sql
```sql
SELECT department_id, AVG(salary) AS average_salary
FROM employees
GROUP BY department_id;
```

This query groups the employees by `department_id` and calculates the average salary for each department.

Filtering Grouped Data: The HAVING Clause

Sometimes, you may want to filter the results of a grouped query based on the aggregate values. For example, you might want to see only the products that have total sales above a certain threshold, or departments with an average salary above a certain amount. For this, you can use the HAVING clause.

Example 1: Filtering Products by Sales

To find products with total sales greater than $10,000, you can use the HAVING clause.

sql

```sql
SELECT product_name, SUM(total_amount) AS total_sales
FROM order_items oi
JOIN products p ON oi.product_id = p.product_id
GROUP BY product_name
HAVING SUM(total_amount) > 10000;
```

This query groups sales by product and filters out any products with total sales below $10,000.

Example 2: Filtering Departments by Average Salary

To find departments where the average salary exceeds $50,000, you can use the HAVING clause.

sql

```sql
SELECT department_id, AVG(salary) AS average_salary
FROM employees
GROUP BY department_id
HAVING AVG(salary) > 50000;
```

Real-World Applications

Let's consider a real-world business scenario. Suppose you are working for an e-commerce company, and your job is to analyze sales data. Here are a few practical queries you might use:

- Find the total sales for each product.
- Calculate the average order value for the last 30 days.
- Count the number of customers who placed more than five orders.
- Find the product with the highest sales in a particular category.

Using aggregation functions like `SUM()`, `AVG()`, `COUNT()`, `MIN()`, and `MAX()` will help you summarize large datasets and extract valuable insights. These functions are essential for reporting, analysis, and decision-making in the business world.

Conclusion

Aggregation is a critical part of SQL, and it plays a central role in summarizing and analyzing data. In this chapter, we've covered the essential aggregate functions—`COUNT()`, `SUM()`, `AVG()`, `MIN()`, and

`MAX()`—and explored how they can be used with the `GROUP BY` and `HAVING` clauses to summarize data and extract meaningful insights. Whether you're calculating total sales, average salaries, or the number of customers in your database, aggregation in SQL allows you to efficiently summarize large datasets and make data-driven decisions.

The next chapter will dive into advanced SQL techniques, such as subqueries, window functions, and more complex joins, which will allow you to handle even more complex data analysis tasks. Stay tuned!

Chapter Five

Joining Tables to Find Meaningful Connections

Introduction to SQL Joins

In the world of relational databases, data is often spread across multiple tables. This makes it necessary to combine data from different tables into a single, cohesive view. This process is known as "joining" tables. SQL provides a variety of `JOIN` operations that allow you to link rows from two or more tables based on a related column, usually a key. Joins are one of the most powerful tools in SQL, enabling you to extract meaningful insights from complex data.

This chapter will dive deep into SQL joins, focusing on understanding when and how to use them, including practical scenarios that demonstrate their power in solving real-world problems.

The Basics of SQL Joins

A JOIN clause in SQL is used to combine rows from two or more tables based on a related column between them. In its simplest form, a join combines data by matching values in specified columns, typically primary and foreign keys.

The syntax for a basic SQL join is:

sql

```sql
SELECT column1, column2
FROM table1
JOIN table2
ON table1.column = table2.column;
```

This query returns data from `table1` and `table2`, where the value in `column` from `table1` matches the value in `column` from `table2`.

Before we dive deeper, it's essential to understand the different types of joins and how each one works.

Types of SQL Joins

There are several types of SQL joins, each with different behavior in terms of how rows are matched between the tables:

1. Inner Join

The **INNER JOIN** is the most commonly used type of join. It returns rows when there is a match in both tables. If there is no match between the tables, no rows are returned. This join is used when you only want to retrieve rows where there is a direct relationship between the tables.

Example:

Let's consider two tables: Customers and Orders.

Customers Table:

CustomerID	CustomerName
1	John Doe
2	Jane Smith
3	Alice Brown

Orders Table:

OrderID	CustomerID	ProductName
101	1	Laptop
102	2	Smartphone
103	4	Headphones

Now, to find all customers who have placed an order, you can use an INNER JOIN:

sql

```
SELECT Customers.CustomerName, Orders.ProductName
FROM Customers
INNER JOIN Orders ON Customers.CustomerID = Orders.CustomerID;
```

Result:

CustomerName	ProductName
John Doe	Laptop
Jane Smith	Smartphone

Notice that Alice Brown is excluded from the result because she has no matching record in the `Orders` table.

2. Left Join (or Left Outer Join)

The **LEFT JOIN** returns all rows from the left table (the first table in the query) and the matched rows from the right table (the second table). If there is no match, NULL values are returned for columns from the right table.

Example:

sql

```
SELECT Customers.CustomerName, Orders.ProductName
FROM Customers
LEFT JOIN Orders ON Customers.CustomerID =
Orders.CustomerID;
```

Result:

CustomerName	ProductName
John Doe	Laptop
Jane Smith	Smartphone
Alice Brown	NULL

In this case, Alice Brown is included, but since there is no matching order for her, the `ProductName` column contains `NULL`.

3. Right Join (or Right Outer Join)

The **RIGHT JOIN** is the opposite of the LEFT JOIN. It returns all rows from the right table and the matched rows from the left table. If there is no match, NULL values are returned for columns from the left table.

Example:

sql

```sql
SELECT Customers.CustomerName, Orders.ProductName
FROM Customers
RIGHT JOIN Orders ON Customers.CustomerID = Orders.CustomerID;
```

Result:

CustomerName	ProductName
John Doe	Laptop
Jane Smith	Smartphone
Alice Brown	NULL
NULL	Headphones

In this example, the order with `OrderID = 103` is included, even though there is no matching customer in the `Customers` table. Thus, `CustomerName` is returned as `NULL`.

4. Full Outer Join

The **FULL OUTER JOIN** combines the behavior of both **LEFT** and **RIGHT** joins. It returns all rows from both tables, and if there is no match, it fills in the missing data with NULLs.

Example:

sql
```
SELECT Customers.CustomerName, Orders.ProductName
FROM Customers
FULL OUTER JOIN Orders ON Customers.CustomerID = Orders.CustomerID;
```

Result:

CustomerName	ProductName
John Doe	Laptop
Jane Smith	Smartphone
Alice Brown	NULL
NULL	Headphones

This time, both unmatched rows from both tables are included. Alice Brown, who did not place an order, has a NULL value for `ProductName`, and the order with no customer has a NULL value for `CustomerName`.

Using Joins in Real-World Scenarios

Let's now look at some practical scenarios where you can use SQL joins to solve real-world business problems:

Scenario 1: Customer Orders Analysis

You work for an e-commerce company that tracks customer orders in two separate tables: `Customers` and `Orders`. You need to generate a report that lists all customers along with the products they have ordered.

1. **Requirement:** Fetch all customers who have placed an order, including those who haven't made a purchase yet.
2. **Solution:** You can use a **LEFT JOIN** to get all customers and their orders.

sql
```
SELECT Customers.CustomerName, Orders.ProductName
FROM Customers
LEFT JOIN Orders ON Customers.CustomerID = Orders.CustomerID;
```

This query returns a list of customers and the products they've ordered, including those who have made no purchase (where `ProductName` is `NULL`).

Scenario 2: Finding Customers with Multiple Orders

Now, let's say you need to identify customers who have ordered multiple products in the past month.

1. **Requirement:** Fetch customers who placed more than one order in the last month.
2. **Solution:** Use an **INNER JOIN** between `Customers` and `Orders` to match only customers who have made multiple purchases.

sql

```sql
SELECT Customers.CustomerName,
COUNT(Orders.OrderID) AS NumberOfOrders
FROM Customers
INNER JOIN Orders ON Customers.CustomerID =
Orders.CustomerID
WHERE Orders.OrderDate BETWEEN '2024-10-01' AND
'2024-10-31'
GROUP BY Customers.CustomerName
HAVING COUNT(Orders.OrderID) > 1;
```

This query retrieves customers who placed multiple orders within a specific time range.

Scenario 3: Product Sales Insights

You need to analyze which products are popular among your customers. The `Orders` table includes product information, and the `Customers` table holds demographic details.

1. **Requirement:** Fetch the total number of orders per product along with customer details.
2. **Solution:** Use an **INNER JOIN** to combine both tables and aggregate the data.

sql

```sql
SELECT Orders.ProductName, COUNT(Orders.OrderID) AS TotalOrders
FROM Orders
INNER JOIN Customers ON Orders.CustomerID = Customers.CustomerID
GROUP BY Orders.ProductName;
```

This query gives you a summary of how many times each product has been ordered, helping you determine which products are bestsellers.

Optimizing Joins for Performance

While SQL joins are powerful, using them incorrectly can result in poor performance. Here are a few tips to optimize queries involving joins:

Use appropriate indexing: Index the columns that are frequently used in JOIN conditions. This improves query performance by speeding up the lookup of matching rows.

sql

```sql
CREATE INDEX idx_customer_id ON Orders(CustomerID);
```

1.
2. **Limit the number of rows returned**: Always use the WHERE clause to filter the data before performing the join. This reduces the number of rows to join and speeds up the process.

Use EXPLAIN: SQL provides an EXPLAIN keyword that shows the execution plan of a query, helping you understand how it's being executed. Use this to identify potential bottlenecks.

sql

```
EXPLAIN SELECT * FROM Customers INNER JOIN Orders
ON Customers.CustomerID = Orders.CustomerID;
```

Conclusion

SQL joins are essential for working with relational databases, enabling you to combine and analyze data spread across multiple tables. Whether you're using an **INNER JOIN** to find related data, a **LEFT JOIN** to include all records from one table, or a **FULL OUTER JOIN** to combine everything, understanding how and when to use each type is crucial for efficient data manipulation.

By applying joins in real-world scenarios like customer orders, sales insights, or product analysis, you can gain meaningful insights that drive business decisions. Always remember to optimize your joins for performance to handle large datasets efficiently.

Chapter Six

SQL Best Practices for Efficiency and Security

SQL (Structured Query Language) is the cornerstone of relational database management systems (RDBMS), empowering developers and database administrators to efficiently store, manipulate, and retrieve data.

However, as databases grow in size and complexity, poor practices in writing SQL queries can severely degrade performance and, more importantly, compromise security.

In this chapter, we will explore some of the best practices for writing efficient SQL queries and ensuring database security.

We will also address how these practices can be applied in real-world scenarios, making the topic highly practical for both beginners and professionals.

1. Writing Efficient SQL Queries

Efficient SQL queries are critical for optimizing the performance of your database. Whether you're working with small or large datasets, inefficient queries can lead to slower response times and increased resource consumption, potentially affecting the performance of your application.

Here are the key practices for writing efficient SQL queries:

a. Use Selective Queries with WHERE Clause

A common mistake in SQL is writing queries that return more data than necessary. This not only wastes resources but also makes it difficult to manage data.

Example:

sql

```
-- Inefficient Query:
SELECT * FROM customers;
```

```
== Efficient Query:
SELECT customer_id, customer_name, email FROM
customers WHERE active = 1;
```

In the inefficient query, the use of `SELECT *` retrieves all columns from the `customers` table, which is unnecessary when you only need specific fields. By using the `WHERE` clause to filter the data, we are also limiting the number of rows returned.

Best Practice: Always specify only the columns you need, and filter data using `WHERE` to avoid unnecessary data retrieval.

b. Use Indexing for Faster Querying

Indexes are one of the most effective ways to speed up database queries, especially when working with large datasets. An index allows the database to find rows much faster by providing a quick lookup based on specific columns.

For example, if you often query by the `customer_id` in the `customers` table, creating an index on this column will make queries that filter by `customer_id` significantly faster.

Example:

sql

```
-- Creating an index on customer_id:
CREATE INDEX idx_customer_id ON
customers(customer_id);
```

Indexes improve read operations, but they come with a trade-off. They slow down write operations (INSERT, UPDATE, DELETE) because the index must be updated every time the data in the indexed column changes. Therefore, it's essential to index columns that are frequently used in search conditions (`WHERE` clauses), sorting (`ORDER BY`), and join operations.

Best Practice: Use indexes wisely on columns that are frequently queried but avoid over-indexing.

c. Avoid Using Subqueries When Possible

Subqueries (queries inside queries) can sometimes lead to poor performance, especially if the subquery is executed multiple times. In many cases, joins can be used to achieve the same result more efficiently.

Example:

sql

```sql
-- Inefficient Query with Subquery:
SELECT customer_name FROM customers WHERE
customer_id IN (SELECT customer_id FROM orders
WHERE order_date = '2023-01-01');

-- More Efficient Query with Join:
SELECT c.customer_name
FROM customers c
JOIN orders o ON c.customer_id = o.customer_id
WHERE o.order_date = '2023-01-01';
```

Using a join in the second query is generally more efficient than using a subquery, as the database engine can optimize the join execution plan more effectively.

Best Practice: Use joins instead of subqueries when possible, as joins tend to be more efficient in most RDBMS.

d. Use Limit and Pagination for Large Datasets

When dealing with large datasets, you should always paginate your queries to avoid retrieving excessive amounts of data in a single query. Pagination helps reduce the load on the database and provides a better experience for users.

Example: sql

```
-- Fetching records in pages of 10 rows:
SELECT * FROM products LIMIT 10 OFFSET 0;   -- First page
SELECT * FROM products LIMIT 10 OFFSET 10;  -- Second page
SELECT * FROM products LIMIT 10 OFFSET 20;  -- Third page
```

The `LIMIT` clause limits the number of rows returned by the query, while the `OFFSET` clause skips a specified number of rows.

Best Practice: Use pagination when displaying large sets of data, such as in search results or user listings, to ensure that your application performs efficiently.

2. Optimizing Complex Queries

In real-world applications, queries can become more complex, involving multiple joins, aggregations, and conditions. It's essential to optimize these queries for both speed and readability.

a. Avoid Using Wildcards with LIKE

Using the `LIKE` operator with wildcards (%) at the beginning of a string can severely degrade query performance because it requires a full table scan to find matching rows.

Example:

sql

```sql
-- Inefficient Query with Leading Wildcard:
SELECT * FROM products WHERE product_name LIKE '%book%';

-- Efficient Query with Trailing Wildcard:
SELECT * FROM products WHERE product_name LIKE 'book%';
```

If possible, avoid using a wildcard at the beginning of the search term. This ensures the database can use indexes and retrieve results faster.

b. Use Grouping and Aggregation Wisely

When using aggregation functions like `SUM()`, `COUNT()`, and `AVG()`, make sure to use them on indexed columns or in conjunction with appropriate filtering (`WHERE`) to limit the dataset before aggregation.

Example:

sql

```sql
-- Efficient Query with Grouping:
SELECT product_category, COUNT(*) as total_products
FROM products
WHERE active = 1
GROUP BY product_category;
```

By limiting the rows to only active products with `WHERE active = 1`, we reduce the dataset before performing the aggregation, which leads to improved query performance.

3. SQL Security Best Practices

Database security is critical in preventing unauthorized access, data leaks, and potential attacks. In this section, we will cover some essential best practices for securing your SQL queries and database access.

a. Use Parameterized Queries

One of the most significant security threats in SQL is SQL injection, where malicious users can insert harmful

SQL code into your queries. This can allow attackers to view, modify, or delete data in your database. To prevent SQL injection, always use parameterized queries instead of dynamic SQL.

Example:

sql

```
# Vulnerable Query (SQL Injection):
cursor.execute("SELECT * FROM users WHERE username = '" + user_input + "' AND password = '" + password_input + "'");

# Secure Query (Parameterized):
cursor.execute("SELECT * FROM users WHERE username = %s AND password = %s", (user_input, password_input));
```

By using parameterized queries, the database engine will treat user inputs as data rather than executable code, thus preventing SQL injection attacks.

Best Practice: Always use parameterized queries, whether you're using raw SQL or an ORM (Object-Relational Mapper) like Django ORM or SQLAlchemy.

b. Principle of Least Privilege

Grant database access based on the principle of least privilege (PoLP). This means users and applications should only have the minimum level of access necessary to perform their job functions.

For example, if a user only needs read access to the database, do not grant them write or administrative privileges. Use roles and permissions to manage access levels and ensure sensitive data is protected.

Example:

sql

```
-- Creating a read-only user:
GRANT SELECT ON database_name.* TO 'read_only_user'@'localhost';
```

This ensures that the user can only read data but not modify it.

c. Encrypt Sensitive Data

For highly sensitive data such as passwords and personal information, always use encryption techniques to ensure the data is not readable by unauthorized individuals.

Example:

sql

```sql
-- Storing a hashed password:
INSERT INTO users (username, password_hash) VALUES
('user1', SHA2('password123', 256));
```

For passwords, it is recommended to use a strong hashing algorithm like bcrypt, scrypt, or Argon2, which are designed to be slow and computationally expensive to thwart brute-force attacks.

Best Practice: Always hash and salt passwords, and encrypt sensitive data before storing it in your database.

d. Regular Backups and Updates

Regular database backups are essential to ensure that you can recover your data in case of an emergency or a security breach. Additionally, keep your database software and server up to date with security patches to avoid vulnerabilities.

Example:

bash

```
# Regular backup of MySQL database:
mysqldump -u root -p my_database > my_database_backup.sql
```

Best Practice: Implement automated backups and ensure that your database management system (DBMS) is regularly updated to the latest version.

Conclusion

SQL is a powerful language that enables developers to manage large volumes of data, but with great power comes great responsibility. By adhering to SQL best practices for efficiency and security, you can ensure that your queries run smoothly and your data remains protected from unauthorized access. Always aim to write efficient, clean, and secure SQL queries that will scale as your application grows. Remember to periodically review your queries and security protocols as your system evolves to keep your databases running optimally and safely.

Chapter Seven

Advanced SQL Techniques

SQL is a powerful language for interacting with relational databases. As you move from simple queries to more complex scenarios, you'll encounter advanced SQL techniques that can drastically improve your productivity, database performance, and maintainability.

This chapter will focus on three advanced SQL techniques: **Views**, **Stored Procedures**, and **Triggers**. We'll explore each of these concepts, provide practical examples, and explain their significance in real-world scenarios.

By the end of this chapter, you will have a deeper understanding of how to leverage these tools for more efficient database management and automation.

1. What Are Views?

A **view** in SQL is essentially a virtual table that allows you to present data in a specific format without modifying the underlying table structure. Views are especially useful when you need to provide a simplified, restricted, or aggregated version of data from one or more tables.

Views allow users to query data as though they were querying a table, while hiding complex joins, calculations, or sensitive data.

Why Use Views?

- **Abstraction**: You can simplify complex queries by creating views that encapsulate complicated logic. Users can query a view as if it were a regular table, saving time and effort.
- **Security**: You can hide sensitive data by providing users with access to a view instead of the underlying table. For instance, you can create a view that excludes certain columns, such as passwords or credit card numbers.

- **Reusability**: Views enable you to reuse SQL logic across multiple queries, improving maintainability.
- **Data Aggregation**: Views are great for aggregating data, performing calculations, or joining multiple tables into a cohesive structure for reporting.

Creating a View

Creating a view is simple. The basic syntax is:

sql

```sql
CREATE VIEW view_name AS
SELECT column1, column2, ...
FROM table_name
WHERE condition;
```

For example, let's say you have an `orders` table that contains information about customer orders, and a `customers` table with customer details. You frequently need to retrieve a list of orders along with customer names. Rather than writing the same complex query every time, you can create a view:

sql
```
CREATE VIEW customer_orders AS
SELECT customers.name, orders.order_id, orders.total_price
FROM orders
JOIN customers ON orders.customer_id = customers.customer_id;
```

Now, whenever you need to retrieve customer order details, you can query the `customer_orders` view as if it were a regular table:

sql
```
SELECT * FROM customer_orders;
```

Updating and Deleting Views

While views simplify data access, it's important to understand their limitations. You can't update or delete data directly through a view if the view involves multiple tables or aggregations. However, you can modify the underlying tables directly. In some databases, you can make a view **updatable** by ensuring it involves only one table and doesn't contain complex functions or joins.

To drop a view, use the following syntax:

sql
```
DROP VIEW view_name;
```

Real-World Scenario: Reporting Dashboard

Imagine you're building a reporting dashboard for an online store. You have several tables: `orders`, `products`, `customers`, and `order_items`. Instead of querying multiple tables and performing complex joins every time, you can create views for specific reports.

For example, you could create a view for total sales by product:

sql
```
CREATE VIEW sales_by_product AS
SELECT products.product_name,
SUM(order_items.quantity) AS total_sales
FROM order_items
JOIN products ON order_items.product_id = products.product_id
GROUP BY products.product_name;
```

Now, you can quickly retrieve sales data for all products by querying the view:

sql
```
SELECT * FROM sales_by_product;
```

This approach speeds up reporting and makes it easier to maintain.

2. What Are Stored Procedures?

A **stored procedure** is a set of SQL statements that can be executed as a single unit. Stored procedures are stored in the database and can be invoked by an application or user whenever needed. They allow you to encapsulate business logic and complex operations in a reusable and efficient way. Stored procedures can accept parameters, perform operations (such as inserts, updates, deletes), and return results.

Why Use Stored Procedures?

- **Performance**: Stored procedures are precompiled, meaning they can execute more quickly than running individual queries. This is because the database engine doesn't need to parse and optimize the SQL each time the procedure is called.

- **Reusability**: By encapsulating business logic in stored procedures, you can reuse the logic across multiple applications or queries.
- **Security**: Stored procedures can help prevent SQL injection attacks because the queries are precompiled. Users don't need to input SQL directly, minimizing the risk of malicious code execution.
- **Maintainability**: If you need to update business logic, you can modify the stored procedure in one place, rather than updating every query that implements the logic.

Creating a Stored Procedure

The basic syntax for creating a stored procedure is as follows:

sql

```sql
CREATE PROCEDURE procedure_name (parameters)
BEGIN
    -- SQL statements
END;
```

For example, let's create a stored procedure to insert a new customer into the `customers` table:

sql

```sql
CREATE PROCEDURE AddCustomer (IN first_name VARCHAR(50), IN last_name VARCHAR(50), IN email VARCHAR(100))
BEGIN
    INSERT INTO customers (first_name, last_name, email)
    VALUES (first_name, last_name, email);
END;
```

To execute the stored procedure:

sql

```sql
CALL AddCustomer('John', 'Doe', 'john.doe@example.com');
```

Real-World Scenario: Automating Report Generation

Let's say you need to generate monthly sales reports that summarize the total sales, number of orders, and average order value. You could write a stored procedure that runs all the necessary calculations and returns a report:

sql

```sql
CREATE PROCEDURE GenerateMonthlyReport (IN month INT, IN year INT)
BEGIN
    SELECT SUM(order_items.quantity) AS total_sales,
           COUNT(DISTINCT orders.order_id) AS total_orders,
           AVG(order_items.total_price) AS average_order_value
    FROM orders
    JOIN order_items ON orders.order_id = order_items.order_id
    WHERE MONTH(orders.order_date) = month AND YEAR(orders.order_date) = year;
END;
```

You can call this procedure at the end of each month to generate the report:

```sql
CALL GenerateMonthlyReport(10, 2023);
```

This stored procedure automates the report generation process, reducing the need for manual query execution.

3. What Are Triggers?

A **trigger** is a type of stored procedure that automatically executes (or "fires") when a specific event occurs in the database. Triggers are commonly used for data validation, enforcing business rules, or automating certain tasks. There are several types of triggers, such as **BEFORE**, **AFTER**, and **INSTEAD OF** triggers, which correspond to the timing of when the trigger should execute relative to the triggering event.

Why Use Triggers?

- **Automation:** Triggers can automate repetitive tasks, such as logging changes to a table or sending notifications when certain conditions are met.
- **Data Integrity:** Triggers can enforce rules and

constraints on the data to maintain consistency.

- **Auditing**: Triggers can be used to create an audit trail of changes made to important data, like tracking updates to sensitive information.

Creating a Trigger

The basic syntax for creating a trigger is:

sql

```sql
CREATE TRIGGER trigger_name
AFTER INSERT ON table_name
FOR EACH ROW
BEGIN
    -- SQL statements to execute
END;
```

For example, let's create a trigger that automatically logs changes to the `orders` table whenever a new order is inserted:

sql

```sql
CREATE TRIGGER LogOrderInsert
AFTER INSERT ON orders
FOR EACH ROW
BEGIN
```

```sql
    INSERT INTO order_log (order_id, action, action_date)
    VALUES (NEW.order_id, 'INSERT', NOW());
END;
```

This trigger will insert a record into the `order_log` table whenever a new order is added to the `orders` table.

Real-World Scenario: Automatically Updating Stock Levels

In an e-commerce system, when a customer places an order, the stock level of the ordered product needs to be updated automatically. You can create a trigger to handle this update when a new order is placed:

sql
```
CREATE TRIGGER UpdateStock
AFTER INSERT ON order_items
FOR EACH ROW
BEGIN
    UPDATE products
    SET stock = stock - NEW.quantity
    WHERE product_id = NEW.product_id;
END;
```

This trigger ensures that stock levels are updated automatically every time an order is placed, without requiring manual intervention.

Conclusion

Views, stored procedures, and triggers are essential tools in advanced SQL development. They provide powerful mechanisms for improving performance, enhancing security, and automating complex tasks. By mastering these techniques, you can build more efficient, maintainable, and secure database applications.

In this chapter, we've covered the basics of these advanced SQL concepts and provided practical examples to help you understand their real-world applications. As you continue to work with SQL, you'll find that these tools can make a significant difference in how you manage and interact with your data. Whether you're building a complex reporting system, automating business processes, or ensuring data integrity, views, stored procedures, and triggers are invaluable assets for any database developer.

By incorporating these techniques into your workflow, you can write cleaner, more efficient SQL code that is easier to maintain and scale. And remember, as with any advanced concept, practice is key. Experiment with these features in your own database environment, and soon you'll be able to take full advantage of their power in your applications.

www.ingramcontent.com/pod-product-compliance
Lightning Source LLC
Chambersburg PA
CBHW051914210526
45473CB00006B/2005